INDEX

SAUCES FOR ALL OCCASIONS

SOUPS & MAIN COURSES

Meats

Seafood

Vegetable/vegetarian

This recipe book came about when I realised that a publishing project I'd started almost a year previously was unlikely to see the light of day due to my other commitments. Quite fortuitously, my Rotary Club was looking for an new annual fundraiser and so we agreed to collaborate and complete the book.

As a chef, I had about sixty good recipes I'd developed around local produce - many of which have featured in our restaurants - and when the call went out, the other members of Hervey Bay Sunrise rallied and sent in their own favourites to be included. Together we plan to publish this book each year with a different theme so you can collect and enjoy the foods of the Fraser Coast with us!

The Rotary Club of Hervey Bay Sunrise is one of the service clubs lucky enough to represent the fabulous Fraser Coast - one of the brightest jewels in Queensland's crown - a region serviced by the surrounding primary producers, a large trawler fleet and featuring our famous humpback whales, Fraser Island and the Mary River.

Our Club is best known for it's major projects including the Cruise for Charity, Tour de Bay bike ride, Rotary's Living Expo (in conjunction with our fellow clubs) and many others - we barely have time to breath sometimes - but also for our participation in many of Rotary's programs including Rotary Youth Programme of Enrichment, Rotary Youth Leadership Award, Rotarians Against Malaria, Rotary Australia World Community Services Ltd (most recently the construction of the Forget-me-Not Orphanage in Nepal) and Roadsafe Youth Driver Awareness to name but a few.

Chartered in 1994, we are a mixed club with membership at a fairly steady 50-55 and one of the lowest average ages for a Rotary Club in region 9570. If ever you're in the neighbourhood, feel free to drop in and have breakfast with us each Thursday 6.15am at the Hervey Bay Community Centre (another of our projects!).

Please enjoy these recipes...they have been selected for their ease and simplicity. They have also been tested by Club members during a rigorous social schedule of dinners and BBQ's, all in the name of research of course!

- Craig Winter, President (2012-2013) Rotary Club of Hervey Bay Sunrise

www.herveybaysunrise.org

First published by ArtxDesign Creative Studios in 2012
Copyright 2012 Craig Winter and the Rotary Club of Hervey Bay

Designed and produced by ArtxDesign, Hervey Bay & Maryborough,
Queensland
www.artxdesign.com.au Font: Swiss721 Light 10/14

Winter, Craig, 1967-
Title: Sunrise Over Fraser: Recipes from Hervey Bay

ISBN: 978-0-9806095-2-3

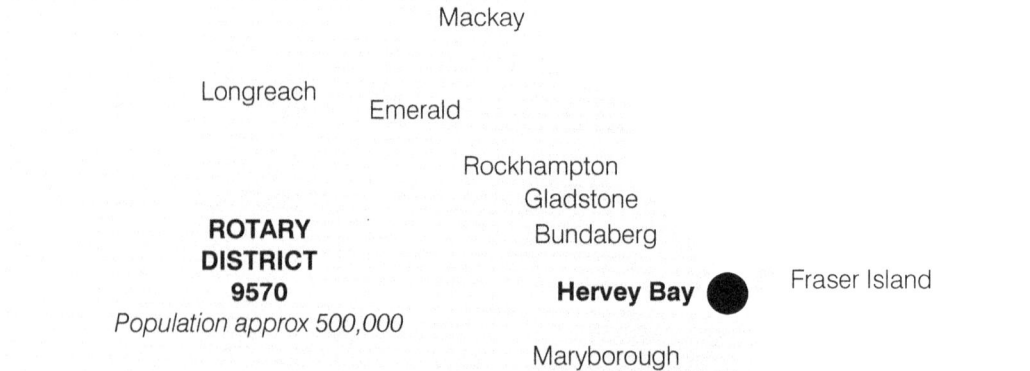

Mackay

Longreach
Emerald

Rockhampton
Gladstone

**ROTARY
DISTRICT
9570**
Population approx 500,000

Bundaberg

Hervey Bay ●   Fraser Island

Maryborough

Queensland

BRISBANE

CAKES, BAKES & DESSERTS

The Rotary Club of Hervey Bay Sunrise was chartered in 1994 as a mixed club comprising around 50 members from all walks of life. We are lucky to be able to call the newly built Hervey Bay Community Centre our home, having played a significant part in sourcing the funding.

It is a five star environmental building, designed in consideration of Hervey Bay's natural environment and climate, and to capture prevailing breezes and harness natural light. It therefore minimize's operating costs for the many social service offices it houses.

This Centre is where the troubled and in-need members of our community can obtain discreet assistance and comfort - but it is also where the joys of our community can be celebrated in style regularly hosting weddings, markets, book sales and much more.

More information can be found at
www.herveybaycommunitycentre.com.au

Hervey Bay, Queensland, Australia is best known as the Whale Watch Capital of the World, and from July through to November each year we are home to hundreds of humpback whales who live here whilst fattening up their newly born calves before the long trip back to Antarctic waters.

sauces for all occasions

Craig's Best BBQ Sauce

I developed this sauce in the 1990s for use in our commercial kitchens and have been using it ever since. It quickly became one of my favourites and can be used thin or thickened with a bit of cornflour. Great on BBQ chicken skewers, beef or pretty much anything.

1/2 cup tomato sauce
2 tablespoons brown sugar
2 tablespoons Worcestershire sauce
1 tablespoon cider vinegar
1 dash Tabasco
1 clove garlic, crushed
1/4 teaspoon Dijon mustard
1/4 teaspoon salt

In a small saucepan over medium heat, stir together the tomato sauce, sugar, Worcestershire sauce, vinegar, Tabasco, garlic, mustard and salt.

Bring to a gentle simmer, then remove from heat and allow to cool slightly before drizzling over your favourite barbecued meats or as a dipping sauce.

TOP TIP
You can coat raw meats lightly in cornflour before browning...then when the sauce is added, it will stick to the meat rather travel straight to the bottom of the plate, and it adds a fantastic texture.

Vaquero Grilling Sauce

A taste of Mexico to use as an overnight marinade on just about any meat, or brush over it on the BBQ.

50g red chillis
1 small tomato
1/4 cup white vinegar
1 tablespoon lemon juice
3 tablespoons cooking oil
1/2 cup onion cut into chunks
2 cloves of garlic
1 handful of fresh coriander
1 teaspoon salt
1 teaspoon black pepper
2 teaspoons of brown sugar
1/2 teaspoon ground cumin

The chillis provide most of the flavour for this recipe so be sure you choose ones you are comfortable with - mild or hot, it's up to you.

Cut the tomato in half and cut out the stem area. Use a spoon to scrape out the seeds and liquid. Chop the remaining tomato flesh into large chunks.

In a food processor, blend the vinegar, lemon juice, and cooking oil for 2-3 seconds. Add the chillis, tomato, onion and coriander and process for another 4-5 seconds, a little longer if using a blender. The sauce should be a bit chunky at this point. Add the remaining ingredients and blend or process until smooth. You can add additional water by the tablespoon, if the sauce needs to be thinned for your needs. Taste the sauce and add more salt as necessary.

Mango & Lime Salsa

Tart up a fresh salad with this fast and easy salsa to add a summery zing...then throw a few prawns on top to really make it special.

2 peeled, pitted and diced mangos
1 diced red onion
1/2 seeded red capsicum
1/3 cup fresh lime juice
1 finely diced jalapeno
1 tablespoon toasted cumin seeds
3 tablespoons fresh, finely chopped coriander

Gently combine and serve.

My Favourite Rémoulade

If you live in Australia, you've probably never made a remoulade and I have to say, you've definitely missed out. Take a batch of this to your next BBQ and watch it disappear!

Can be spooned onto a plate beside any meat but is absolutely fantastic with crumbed fish.

3/4 cup mayonnaise
1 1/2 tablespoons finely chopped bottled gherkins
1 teaspoon finely chopped capers
1 tablespoon lemon juice
1 tablespoon Dijon mustard
2 teaspoons chopped fresh parsley
1/4 teaspoon dried leaf tarragon
Tabasco to taste
Salt to taste

Thoroughly combine the mayonnaise, gherkins, chopped capers, lemon juice, mustard, parsley, and tarragon.

Taste and add Tabasco and salt, if needed.

Cover and refrigerate until serving time.

Super-easy Carbonara

Whip this up in a few minutes for a fresh family favourite.

2 teaspoons olive oil
200g sliced bacon or pancetta, roughly chopped
3 cloves garlic, crushed
2 egg yolks (at room temperature)
2 eggs (at room temperature)
1/2 cup thickened cream
75g parmesan cheese, finely grated

Heat oil in a large, non-stick frying pan over medium heat. Cook bacon or pancetta and garlic for 5 minutes while stirring until crisp. Remove from heat.

Whisk egg yolks, eggs, cream and three-quarters of the parmesan together in a bowl. Season with salt and pepper.

Add egg mixture to bacon in pan and heat gently until it starts to thicken, then just add to your favourite pasta.

Be careful not to overcook or it will scramble.

Fast White Wine Sauce

Take your average piece of chicken, fish or pork up a notch by sauteing in this elegant classic for added flavour and class.

Extra virgin olive oil
1/3 cup finely chopped onion
1/2 cup chicken stock
1/4 cup dry white wine
2 tablespoons white wine vinegar
2 tablespoons butter
2 teaspoons finely chopped fresh chives

Heat a pan to medium-high and lightly coat with extra virgin olive oil. Add onion to pan and sauté for 2 minutes whilst stirring. Stir in chicken broth, white wine, and white wine vinegar then bring to the boil. Cook until reduced to 1/4 cup (about 5 minutes).

Remove from heat; stir in butter and fresh chives before serving.

Tricia's Green Sauce

Use on new potatoes, hard-boiled eggs, beef or fish.

15g each of fresh thyme, chives, oregano, lemon grass, coriander, parsley etc mixed herbs
1 carton (150g/5oz) creme fraiche or sour cream.
1 small onion, finely chopped
150g plain yoghurt
1-2 tablespoons olive oil
1 teaspoon medium-strong mustard
1 drop lemon juice
1/2 teaspoon sugar
Salt and pepper to taste

Rinse herbs, pat dry and remove leaves from stems.
Chop leaves coarsely and puree together with 2 tablespoons creme fraiche in a bowl.

Stir in rest of the creme fraiche, yoghurt, chopped onions, oil and mustard into herb mix then season with lemon juice, sugar, salt and pepper.

Refrigerate until ready to serve.

TOP TIP
Tricia's Green Sauce recipe is perfect for ad-libbing. Experiment with whatever herbs you have in the house and see what happens.

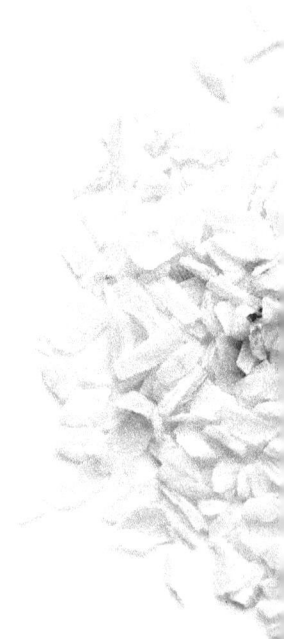

Basic Sweet & Sour Sauce

Another of my commercial sauces designed to be fast and foolproof. Use on the usual chicken and pork dishes, but also fantastic on grilled fish.

1 cup white vinegar
1 cup white sugar
Small tin of pineapple chunks in natural juice
1 tablespoon tomato sauce

Combine vinegar and sugar in a pan and bring to a simmer whilst stirring until is completely dissolved. Take off heat and stir in pineapple, juice and tomato

You can thicken this up with a little cornflour and water if needed.

Being a member of Rotary is more than just breakfast meetings and fundraising. It's also about friendships and enjoying life with like-minded people.

Our members range in age from 30 to 80, and we love getting out amongst the public to provide support, encourage education, and generally make our communities better places to live for everyone.

We have a number of high profile projects each year (Cruise for Charity, Tour de Bay, Rotary Book Sale, Living Expo and others) to raise funds for our programs at local, national and international levels, but we also do many smaller community projects each month and participate along with our local Council, other community services and sporting clubs on a regular basis.

In conjunction with neighbouring Rotary Clubs, we also provide significant funding for major projects such as Variety Sunshine Coaches (left) and share the philosophy of "service above self" as the use of each Rotarian's occupation as an opportunity to serve society.

There are over 1.2 million Rotarians in 33,000 Clubs around the world combining to provide massive assistance to those in need, with our best known project the ongoing eradication of polio. Since 1985, over two billion children around the globe have been vaccinated.

Now we are within two years of eradicating this disease from the world forever.

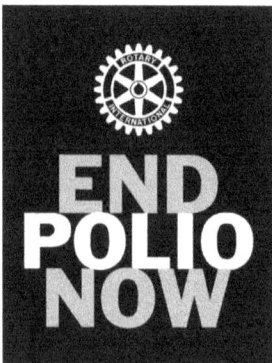

Hervey Bay seafood is recognised as some of the finest in the world, and our large trawler fleet provides us with fresh fish, crabs, prawns and scallops in abundance.

soups & main courses

Coq au Vin

1 1/2 cups peeled baby carrots
3/4 cup chicken stock
1 1/2 tablespoons tomato paste
5 slices thick-cut bacon, cut crosswise into strips
300g small button mushrooms
2 teaspoons minced garlic
2 teaspoons chopped fresh rosemary
2 teaspoons fresh thyme
500g small pickling onions
1 cup dry white wine
1 cooked rotisserie chicken, cut into 8 pieces
3 tablespoons chopped parsley

Place carrots in a microwave-safe bowl with 1/2 cup water; cover bowl with vented plastic wrap and microwave on high 4 to 5 minutes, until cooked but still crisp; drain.

Mix stock and tomato paste in a small cup; set aside.
Meanwhile, in a large, deep pot, cook bacon until crisp then remove with a slotted spoon to a paper towel. Cook mushrooms, garlic, rosemary, and thyme in the leftover bacon oil over medium-high heat for 6 minutes, or until lightly browned. Add onions and continue to cook for another 3 minutes.

Raise heat to high and add wine to deglaze, scraping up browned bits from bottom of the pot with a wooden spoon. When wine boils, add broth mixture, stirring to incorporate.

Add chicken pieces and carrots; bring to a boil, reduce heat to medium-low, cover, and simmer 5 minutes, turning chicken once or twice.

Transfer to a serving platter and sprinkle with bacon and parsley.

San Choy Bow

This is a great dish for summer entertaining. It looks great, tastes great, and is light and healthy.

Pork is the classic meat for this dish, but also good with chicken, turkey or beef instead.

Try serving with a fine-cut, sweet coleslaw on the side.

1 tablespoon peanut oil
1 teaspoon sesame oil
1 clove garlic, crushed
1 tablespoon grated ginger
4 green shallots, chopped
500g lean pork mince
1 red capsicum, finely diced
230g can water chestnuts, roughly chopped
2 tablespoons soy sauce
1 tablespoon oyster sauce
2 tablespoons dry sherry
1 tablespoon fresh coriander (optional)
1 iceberg, cups trimmed and washed

Heat oils on medium heat and add garlic, ginger and shallots, cook for 2 minutes.

Add mince and stir until brown then add capsicum, water chestnuts, soy sauce, oyster sauce and sherry. Simmer for 3 minutes until sauce thickens.

Remove from heat, add coriander.

Mix and serve in lettuce cups. Feel free to top with optional additional cucumber, sprouts etc as you wish.

Aromatic Dark Beef Curry

Quick and easy with very little spice although you can add chilli if you like.

1 kg round (or topside) steak
3 tablespoons of extra virgin olive oil
1 onion, chopped
1 apple, peeled and chopped
1/4 cup chopped raisins
1 1/2 cups chopped dates
2 teaspoons curry powder
2 tablespoons of lemon juice
1 tablespoon of tomato paste
2 teaspoons of Worcestershire sauce
1 tablespoon fruit chutney
1 tablespoon of brown sugar
2 cups of beef stock

Dice the steak into cubes and brown the meat in the pan with the oil.

Add the other ingredients and bring to the boil then immediately reduce heat and simmer covered for 1½ hours or until the meat is tender.

Stir in 2 tablespoons of cornflour and water and keep stirring over medium heat until the mixture bubbles and thickens.

Serve with Henny's Special Saffron Rice.

Henny's Special Saffron Rice

2 1/2 cups Basmati rice
5 cups water
Saffron powder
2 tablespoons ultanas
1 teaspoon salt
2 teaspoons cumin seeds

Combine all ingredients in a large microwave-safe rice cooker and cook on high for 10 minutes.

Take out of microwave and stir through.
Cook for a further 10 mins on high.

This recipe is served with any of your favourite curries.

Bacon Wrapped Quail in Marsala

8 quail
Salt & freshly ground black pepper
1 kg parsnips, peeled, topped
2 tablespoons olive oil
1 small brown onion, halved, finely chopped
1 celery stick, trimmed, finely chopped
1 small carrot, peeled, finely chopped
1 cup fresh breadcrumbs
2 sprigs fresh rosemary, leaves picked
1 lemon, rind finely shredded
500g rindless streaky bacon
3/4 cup marsala

Rinse each quail cavity under cold running water. Pat dry with paper towel (inside and out) and season with salt and pepper.

Cut each parsnip in half lengthways, then each half into 3 equal pieces. Place pieces, in a single layer, in a large roasting pan and drizzle with 1 tablespoon of olive oil. Season with salt and pepper, and set aside.

Preheat oven to 180°C. Heat a large frying pan over medium heat. Add the remaining olive oil. Add onions and cook, stirring, for 3 minutes or until soft then add the celery and carrot, and continue cooking and stirring, for a further 2 minutes.
Combine the breadcrumbs and onion mixture in a large bowl. Add the rosemary and lemon rind. Season with salt and pepper, and stir until well combined. Fill each quail cavity with the seasoning mixture. Wrap a bacon rasher around the middle of each quail and secure with a toothpick. Place the quail on the parsnip in the roasting pan. Bake in preheated oven for 35-40 minutes or until the quail juices run clear when pierced with a skewer in the thickest part of the breast.
Transfer quail to a plate and cover loosely with foil. Place the roasting pan over high heat. Add the marsala, scraping the pan with a flat-bottomed wooden spoon, until it comes to the boil. Boil, stirring occasionally, for 3 minutes or until reduced by half. Season with salt and pepper. Strain through a fine wire sieve into a jug.

Place quail with parsnip on serving plates. Pour over a little of the sauce and serve immediately with a salad.

BBQ Chilli & Sesame Beef with Red Cabbage Slaw

2 tablespoons sesame seeds
2 garlic cloves, peeled
2 teaspoons sambal oelek
1/4 cup soy sauce
1/4 cup caster sugar
1/4 cup white vinegar
2 tablespoons vegetable oil
800g sirloin, thinly sliced
1/4 red cabbage, thinly sliced
3 shallots, trimmed, thinly sliced
3 red radishes, cut into matchsticks

Preheat barbecue to high heat. Place sesame seeds in small frying pan over low heat and cook, stirring, for 1 minute or until toasted. Transfer seeds and garlic to a mortar and pound with a pestle until smooth. Add the sambal oelek, soy sauce, sugar, vinegar and oil, and stir to combine.

Place beef slices in a medium bowl and stir through 1/4 cup of the sesame mixture. Cover with plastic wrap and set aside. Combine cabbage, green onion, radish and half of remaining dressing in a bowl.

Cook beef on barbecue for 1 minute each side or until browned and just cooked. Toss steak in remaining dressing. Divide the cabbage mixture among serving dishes. Top with beef and serve immediately with steamed rice, if desired.

Hervey Bay BBQ Pork Ribs

2/3 cup corn syrup
1/4 cup Worcestershire sauce
1 tablespoon mustard powder
1/4 cup dark brown sugar
1/2 cup beer
2 tablespoons treacle
Few drops of Tabasco sauce
1.5kg pork ribs

Combine corn syrup, Worcestershire sauce, mustard powder, dark brown sugar, beer, treacle and Tabasco. Mix well.

Cut pork ribs into pieces, 3-4 bones per piece. Place ribs in a large plastic container and pour over the syrup mixture, making sure the ribs are well coated. Cover and refrigerate for 2 hours or overnight.

Preheat oven to moderate 180°C. Transfer ribs to a baking dish and drain marinade into a separate small pan. Gently simmer the marinade for 5-10 minutes. Bake ribs for 1 hour 45 minutes until sticky, basting often during cooking.

Serve with Beer Battered Chips and extra sauce.

Chicken & Leek Bake

As a kid I hated leeks and now, with my best leek-eating days behind me, I make this quite often when I'm after something to fortify me on winter nights.

500g potatoes, peeled, cut into 2cm pieces
1/2 cup cream
1 tablespoon olive oil
1 leek, trimmed, halved lengthways, thinly sliced
500g chicken tenderloins, halved crossways
1 1/2 cups chicken stock
1 tablespoon cornflour
3 teaspoons water
1 cup corn kernels
1/4 cup chopped fresh flat leaf parsley
1/4 cup coarsely grated cheddar

Place the potato in a saucepan of lightly salted water and bring to the boil over high heat, cooking for 15 minutes or until tender. Drain and return to the pan, add half of the cream and mash.

Meanwhile, heat the oil in a large non-stick frying pan over medium-high heat. Add the leek and chicken, and cook, stirring often, for 5 minutes. Add the stock then reduce heat to medium. Cook for 10 minutes. Combine the cornflour and water in a small bowl and stir into the mixture. Cook for another 5 minutes or until the mixture thickens. Stir in the corn, parsley and remaining cream. Season to taste.

Preheat grill. Transfer the chicken mixture to a 2 litre baking dish and then spread the mash over chicken, sprinkling with cheddar. Grill until golden on top.

Lemon Chicken Piccata

Lemons and chickens were meant to be together...
a classic combination in many countries.

1/4 cup egg beaten
3 tablespoons lemon juice
1/3 cup whole wheat flour
1/8 teaspoon garlic powder
1/8 teaspoon paprika
4 skinned and boned chicken breast halves
3 tablespoons olive oil
2 chicken stock cubes
1/2 cup hot water
1 tablespoon capers and lemon wedges to garnish

Combine egg and 1 tablespoon lemon juice in a small bowl; beat well.

Combine flour, garlic powder and paprika in a small bowl; stir well.

Pound each chicken breast between two sheets of waxed paper until uniform in thickness. About 1/4 inch thick is best.

Dip chicken in egg mixture; dredge in flour mixture. Brown chicken in olive oil in a large skillet over medium high heat 2 to 3 minutes on each side.

Dissolve stock cubes in hot water then add mixture and 2 tablespoons lemon juice to skillet with the chicken. Bring to boil; cover, reduce heat and simmer 15 to 20 minutes or until chicken is done. Garnish with capers and lemon wedges.

Orange Chicken LaTosca

1 tablespoon olive oil
1 1/2 teaspoon dried thyme
1/2 teaspoon salt
1/4 teaspoon white or black pepper
500g boneless, skinless chicken breasts
2 small to medium oranges
3 tablespoons rice-wine vinegar
2 tablespoons honey

In a glass dish, mix together the oil, thyme, salt, and pepper for a quick marinade.

Place the chicken flat on a cutting board, remove any fat, and slice each breast into quarters so that you have 3cm thick strips. Add the meat to the marinade and toss to coat. Cover and place in the fridge for at least 15 minutes.

Zest the orange using a grater then using a sharp knife, cut away the remaining peel and pith, and holding the fruit over a bowl to catch the juice, cut sections from the orange, working in a V fashion to cut away any membrane. Reserve the fruit and juice for the sauce.

Preheat a nonstick skillet to moderate heat.
Spray with nonstick cooking spray, then add the chicken once the pan is hot. Discard the marinade. Cook the chicken until firm and no longer pink, about 5 minutes.

While the meat is cooking, place the vinegar and honey in a small saucepan and bring to a boil. Lower the heat and simmer until the mixture is reduced by half. Add the orange, juice, and the zest to the sauce, stir, and remove from the heat.

Divide the chicken onto 4 plates and pour the sauce over the meat.

Balsamic Lamb

1/4 cup balsamic vinegar
2 tablespoons olive oil
2 tablespoons rosemary leaves, roughly chopped
550g lamb loin fillets
Olive oil cooking spray
6 baby eggplant, trimmed, halved lengthways
100g baby spinach
250g hommus dip, to serve

Combine vinegar, oil, rosemary and salt and pepper in a shallow ceramic dish. Add lamb. Turn to coat. Cover and refrigerate for 1 hour (or longer if time permits).

Preheat a barbecue plate on medium/high heat. Remove lamb from marinade. Barbecue for 5 to 6 minutes each side for medium or until cooked to your liking. Transfer to a plate. Cover with foil and set aside for 5 minutes to rest.

Spray eggplant with oil. Barbecue for 1 to 2 minutes each side or until tender.

Slice lamb. Arrange spinach on a serving platter. Top with eggplant and lamb. Season with salt and pepper. Serve with hommus.

Kangaroo Macadamia Salad & Mustard Dressing

1/2 teaspoon lemon myrtle seasoning
2 rosemary sprigs, leaves picked
3 garlic cloves
1 tablespoon macadamia oil
2 tablespoons chopped fresh thyme
600g kangaroo loin fillets
2 cups each baby spinach & rocket leaves
1/2 red onion, thinly sliced
1 red capsicum, thinly sliced
1/2 cup roasted macadamia halves

Honey mustard dressing
2 teaspoon honey mustard
2 tablespoons white wine vinegar
1/3 cup macadamia oil

Using a mortar and pestle, pound the lemon myrtle, rosemary leaves, garlic cloves and macadamia oil to a paste. Transfer to a bowl and stir in the spice mix. Add the kangaroo fillets and turn to coat in the spice mixture. Cover with plastic wrap and chill for at least 1 hour, preferably overnight.

Heat chargrill pan or barbecue over high heat. When hot, add the kangaroo fillets and cook for 2-3 minutes each side for medium-rare or until the fillets are cooked to your liking. Transfer to a plate and rest, covered loosely with foil, for 5 minutes.

For the dressing, whisk the mustard, vinegar and oil in a bowl until combined.

Combine spinach and rocket in a large bowl. Slice the fillets 1cm thick and scatter over the leaves with the onion, capsicum and macadamias. Drizzle with dressing and serve immediately.

Asparagus with Prosciutto

6 slices prosciutto, thinly sliced lengthways
2 bunches asparagus, woody ends trimmed

Wrap a slice of prosciutto around an asparagus spear. Repeat with remaining prosciutto and asparagus.
Preheat barbecue on high. Cook asparagus on barbecue, turning occasionally, for 5 minutes or until just tender. Serve on a platter with baby potato rosemary skewers.

TOP TIP

When buying asparagus, choose firm, bright green stalks with tight tips. If stems are tough, use a vegetable peeler to remove the outer layer.
Wrapped in plastic, they will keep in the fridge for three to four days.

Sicilian Barbecued Fish with Chickpea Puree

1 whole garlic bulb
1/3 cup olive oil
2 x 400g cans chickpeas, rinsed, drained
1/2 cup chicken stock
1/4 cup pine nuts
12 drained anchovy fillets (optional)
3 x 200g punnets grape tomatoes
4 skin-on white fish fillets
1/4 cup currants
1/3 cup fresh mint leaves
1/3 cup fresh continental parsley leaves

Preheat oven to 180°C. Trim 5mm from the top of the garlic bulb. Drizzle over a little of the oil and rub to coat.
Bake for 50 minutes or until soft and golden.

Peel the skin from 5 garlic cloves. Discard skin. Place the garlic flesh in the bowl of a food processor. Add the chickpeas and stock, and process until smooth. Transfer to a microwave-safe bowl. Taste and season with salt and pepper. Cover with plastic wrap.

Place the pine nuts in a large frying pan over medium heat. Cook, stirring often, for 3 minutes or until golden. Transfer to a bowl.

Reserve 3 teaspoons of the oil and heat the remaining oil in the frying pan over medium heat. Add the anchovies and cook, stirring, for 1 minute. Add the tomatoes. Reduce heat to medium-low and cook, stirring occasionally, for 8 minutes or until the tomatoes are soft.

Preheat a barbecue flat plate on medium-high. Brush both sides of the fish with the reserved oil. Season with salt and pepper. Add to the barbecue and cook for 2-3 minutes each side or until golden and the fish flakes when tested with a fork in the thickest part.

Meanwhile, heat the chickpea puree in the microwave on high/800watts/100%, stirring once, for 3 minutes or until heated through.

Add the pine nuts, currants, mint and parsley to the tomato mixture. Season with pepper. Toss to combine.
Divide puree and fish among serving plates. Top with tomato mixture to serve.

Hervey Bay Rissotto

1 1/2 litres fish or vegetable stock
500g fresh calamari, cleaned
500g green prawns
2 tablespoons extra virgin olive oil
1 large onion, chopped finely
2 cloves garlic, chopped finely
2 cups arborio rice
Pinch of saffron threads
3/4 cup dry white wine
3/4 cup tomato purée
2 teaspoons finely grated lemon rind
2 tablespoons finely chopped fresh parsley

Bring the stock to a gentle simmer in a medium saucepan.

Meanwhile, cut calamari hoods down the centre to open out. Score the inside in a diagonal pattern, then cut into pieces. Shell and de-vein prawns, leaving tails intact.

Heat half the oil in a large, heavy-based pan; cook prawns and calamari over high heat, in batches, until the prawns have just changed colour. Remove from pan.

Heat the remaining oil in the same large, heavy-based pan; add onion and garlic, cook, stirring, until onion is soft. Add rice and saffron, stir to coat well with onion mixture' stirring for 1 minute.

Add wine, simmer, uncovered, until liquid has evaporated. Stir in tomato purée and cook, stirring, for 1 minute.

Add 1/2 cup of the hot stock, stirring, over a medium heat, until the liquid is absorbed. Continue adding stock, 1/2 cup at a time, stirring between each addition, until all but 1/2 cup of the stock has been absorbed (this step should take about 20 minutes). Stir in remaining stock and cover pan with lid, cook for about 5 minutes.

Return the prawns and calamari to rissotto with the lemon rind and parsley; stir in gently.

Brodetto

A traditional Italian seafood stew for all occasions.

4 tablespoons olive oil
1 onion, peeled and chopped
3 celery stalks, chopped
1 carrot, peeled and diced
2 cloves garlic, peeled and chopped
450g Roma tomatoes, peeled and chopped
1 hot, dried chilli pepper, chopped
4 tablespoons finely chopped flat-leaf parsley
1 glass dry white wine
1kg mixed fish fillets (such as bream, snapper or mullet)

Heat olive oil in a large saucepan over a medium heat. Sauté onion, celery, carrot and garlic in the pan for about 5 minutes or until golden brown in colour.

Add tomatoes, dried chilli, parsley and wine, stir mixture well and cook for about 10 minutes until softened. Place the fish carefully on top, pouring over a little water if necessary to just cover the fish.

Cook for 15-20 minutes over low heat, covered, until all the fish is cooked through. Season generously with sea salt and freshly ground black pepper then transfer the soup into bowls and serve each with a slice of toasted ciabatta-style bread.

Hervey Bay Martini

I probably owe someone an apology for this one as I stole the recipe ages ago and can't remember who created it. It's very different, and very tasty.

400g fresh king prawns, peeled and tail intact
Small sandcrab, chopped
250g baby octopus
8 scallops in shell
50ml olive oil
1 clove garlic, crushed
1/4 cup chopped lemon thyme
Salt and pepper, to taste

MARTINI DRESSING
30g pitted green olives, chopped coarsely
Zest and juice of 1 lemon
30ml citrus flavoured vodka
10ml vermouth
100ml olive oil
1 cup of crushed ice
Extra 1/4 cup pitted green olives

Clean and prepare the seafood. Toss olive oil, garlic and thyme with the mixed seafood.

Season with salt and pepper.

Cook on a heated oiled barbecue plate or grill, over a high heat for 10 minutes or until seafood is just cooked through.

To make martini dressing, place green olives, zest and juice of lemon, crushed ice, vodka, vermouth and olive oil in a cocktail shaker. Shake well, then strain over the cooked seafood and sprinkle with extra olive oil, lemon and pepper to garnish.

Balsamic Glazed Cracked Pepper Salmon

1 tablespoon honey
1 tablespoon olive oil
1/3 cup of balsamic vinegar
Red pepper flakes, to taste
Sea salt and cracked black pepper, to taste
4 salmon fillets

Heat oil in a large skillet over medium-high heat. Season both sides of salmon with salt and cracked pepper. Add salmon to skillet and cook for 1 to 2 minutes per side, until golden brown.

Meanwhile, in a small bowl, whisk together vinegar and honey. Add vinegar mixture to skillet and simmer until fish is fork-tender and liquid reduces and thickens, about 5 minutes. For a thicker, reduced sauce, simmer for an additional 5 to 10 minutes.

Seafood Ravioli with Sesame

This is a great recipe when you want to make a little more effort for your dinner parties. All I can say is that it's worth it!

250g green prawns, peeled, chopped coarsely
100g fish fillets, chopped coarsely
2 cloves garlic, crushed
2cm piece ginger, grated finely
1/2 teaspoon sesame oil
12 fresh scallops on the shell
24 wonton wrappers
1 egg white, beaten lightly
1 cup loosely packed coriander leaves
2 shallots, sliced thinly

SESAME DRESSING
2 tablespoons kecap manis
2 tablespoons rice wine vinegar
1/4 teaspoon sesame oil
1 long red chilli, sliced thinly

Process the prawns, fish, garlic, ginger and sesame oil until almost smooth. Remove the scallops from the shells.

Place a heaped teaspoon of the prawn filling in the centre of 12 wonton wrappers, then one scallop on top of the filling. Lightly brush edges with egg white. Place another wrapper on top, pressing edges firmly to seal.

Using the blunt edge of a 5.5cm round cutter, gently press around the filling to seal. Then, using a 7cm cutter, cut the wontons into rounds; discard excess wonton pastry. Transfer to tray lined with a tea towel.

For the sesame dressing, combine all ingredients in a screw-top jar; shake well.

Cook the ravioli, in two batches, in a large saucepan of simmering, well-salted water; simmer, uncovered, for about 3 minutes or until seafood is just cooked through. Remove the ravioli from the pan with a slotted spoon; drain on absorbent paper.

Divide the ravioli among serving plates, drizzle with the sesame dressing and top with combined coriander and shallots.

Prawn Saganaki

Saganaki = small Greek frying pan.

500g raw king prawns
3 tablespoons olive oil
1 onion, chopped
1 teaspoon freshly chopped parsley
1 cup white wine
400g tin chopped tomatoes, drained
1 clove garlic, finely chopped
200g feta cheese, cubed

Place the prawns in a pot and add enough water to cover them. Boil for 5 minutes, then drain.

Heat about 2 tablespoons of oil in a saucepan. Add the onion and cook, stirring until the onions are soft. Mix in the parsley, wine, tomatoes, garlic and remaining olive oil.

Simmer, stirring occasionally, for about 30 minutes, or until the sauce is thickened.

While the sauce is simmering, the prawns should have become cool enough to handle. First remove the legs by pinching them, and then pull off the shells, leaving the head and tail on.

When the sauce has thickened, stir in the prawns. Bring to a simmer, and cook for about 5 minutes.

Add the feta cheese and remove from the heat. Let stand until the cheese starts to melt.

Pam's Thai-style Green Curry

Feel free to substitute chicken or beef for the prawns in this dish.

1 tablespoon of oil
3 tablespoons green curry paste
2 tablespoons fish sauce
1 teaspoon sugar
400ml coconut milk
300g green prawns, peeled and de-veined
Your choice of vegetables ie carrots, zucchini, cauliflower, broccoli, snow peas, capsicum

In a wok heat olive oil and add the green curry paste.

Simmer on low heat for 5 minutes, then add prawns and stir constantly for 3 minutes or until cooked through. Add the fish sauce, sugar and coconut milk and stir until combined. Add chopped vegetables, cover and simmer for 5 further minutes.

Serve immediately over hot fluffy jasmine rice.

TOP TIP
Make your own fresh green curry paste:

1/2 teaspoon ground cumin
1 1/2 teaspoons of ground coriander
2 or 3 green chillies
3 teaspoons of minced ginger
4 teaspoons of minced garlic
3 lemongrass stalks, finely chopped
6 heaped tablespoons of freshly chopped coriander
Zest of 1 lime
Juice of 2 limes
2 tablespoons of oil

Add all the ingredients into a food processor and blend to form a thick smooth paste or chop all the paste ingredients very finely by hand and mix to blend.

Sweet Chilli Seafood Melange

Using some of the best seafood Hervey Bay has to offer.

1 tablespoon oil
2 cloves garlic, chopped
3cm piece ginger, finely shredded
8 large prawns, peeled and de-veined
2 Moreton Bay bug tails, meat removed and halved
8 Hervey Bay scallops
2 tablespoons sweet chilli sauce
1 tablespoon oyster sauce
2 teaspoons fish sauce
2 shallots, chopped.
Steamed jasmine rice to serve

Heat oil in a wok or large frying pan over medium high heat and cook garlic and ginger for 1-2 minutes or until fragrant.

Add prawns, and toss for 1 minute; stir in bug meat and cook a further 2 minutes.

Finally, add scallops and sauces and stir-fry until seafood is cooked and sauce has thickened and is sticky.

Serve with steamed rice and topped with shallots.

Canton Prawn & Pork Dumplings

I have made far more siu mai *than I care to remember but I still love eating them. Once made by street vendors on the side of the road, and now in all the finest restaurants around the world.*

125g pork mince
1 cup chopped watercress
110g water chestnuts, drained and chopped
2 spring onions, chopped
1 tablespoon oyster sauce
1 1/2 tablespoons sesame oil
1 clove garlic, crushed
1 teaspoon soy sauce
Pinch ground white pepper
Pinch salt
40 wonton wrappers
500g raw prawns, peeled and de-veined
Oil for shallow frying

In a large bowl, combine the pork, watercress, water chestnuts, spring onion, oyster sauce, sesame oil, garlic, soy sauce, white pepper and salt and mix together well.

Place 1/2 teaspoonful of filling onto each wrapper. Place 1 prawn on the filling, slightly wetting the edge of the wrapper with water, fold over and pinch with your fingers to form a tight seal all the way around. Ensure no air is trapped inside the sealed wrapper.

Pan fry the dumplings in a large frying pan over medium heat with a little oil for 15 minutes, turning over halfway through.
Alternately, place them in a pot of boiling water for 10 minutes; drain and serve in hot chicken stock or simply steam in bamboo baskets.

Fraser Island Seafood Paella

You will probably never have the opportunity to make this on the beach looking out over a Fraser Island sunset, but just imagine it...

1 tablespoon olive oil
100g chorizo sausage, sliced
1 medium brown onion, sliced
2 cloves garlic, crushed
1 medium red capsicum, sliced
2 cups medium grain white rice
1/4 teaspoon turmeric
1 cup fish stock
1 cup water
1 cup frozen peas
400g can tomatoes, drained, crushed
500g marinara mix
300g firm white fish fillets, chopped
Lemon wedges to serve

Heat the oil in a heated large non-stick frying pan. Add the chorizo, onion and garlic; cook, stirring, until browned.

Add the capsicum, rice and turmeric, cook, stirring, for 1 minute. Stir in the fish stock, water, peas and tomatoes.

Place the seafood over the top of the rice mixture; cover the pan and cook over a low heat for about 6 minutes or until the rice is tender and the seafood is cooked through.

Serve with lemon wedges.

Cedar Planked Salmon

For something completely different, try this on the BBQ with whatever fish is available, but salmon is best.

2 untreated cedar planks, just long enough to fit fillets
1/3 cup vegetable oil
1 1/2 tablespoons rice vinegar
1 teaspoon sesame oil
1/3 cup soy sauce
1/4 cup chopped green onions
1 tablespoon grated fresh ginger
1 teaspoon minced garlic
2 salmon fillets, skin removed

Soak the cedar planks for at least 1 hour in warm water. Soak longer if you have time.

In a shallow dish, stir together the vegetable oil, rice vinegar, sesame oil, soy sauce, green onions, ginger, and garlic. Place the salmon fillets in the marinade and turn to coat. Cover and marinate for at least 15 minutes, or up to one hour.

Preheat the BBQ to medium heat. Place the planks on the grate. The boards are ready when they start to smoke and crackle just a little.

Place the salmon fillets onto the planks and discard the marinade. Cover, and grill for about 20 minutes. Fish is done when you can flake it with a fork. It will continue to cook after you remove it from the grill.

Consider serving with an Asian-inspired rice dish.

Classic Poached Salmon

A simple dinner party classic.

4 salmon fillets, skin removed
1 lemon, sliced
1 small brown onion, quartered
2 bay leaves
1/2 teaspoon whole black peppercorns
Stems of parsley

Remove pin bones from the salmon with tweezers. Choose large saute pan with lid which will comfortably fit the salmon fillets; place salmon in base.

Add the lemon, onion, bay leaves, peppercorns and parsley stems; cover with water. Cook covered over medium heat for about 2-5 minutes or until cooked to your liking.

Lift out carefully with a slotted spoon.

Transfer to plate and cover to keep warm.

Perfect with Tricia's Green Sauce.

Spicy Prawn & Cod Soup

1/2 onion, chopped
1 clove garlic, minced
1 tablespoon chilli powder
1 1/2 cups chicken stock
2 green chillis, chopped
1 teaspoon ground cumin
1 1/2 cups tinned peeled and diced tomatoes
1/2 cup chopped green capsicum
1/2 cup prawns
250g cod fillets
3/4 cup plain nonfat yoghurt

Spray a large saucepan with the vegetable cooking spray over medium high heat. Add the onions and saute, stirring often, for about 5 minutes. Add the garlic and chilli powder and saute for 2 more minutes.

Then add the chicken stock, chilli and cumin, stirring well. Bring to the boil, reduce heat to low, cover and simmer for 20 minutes.

Next, add the tomatoes, green capsicum, prawns and cod. Return to the boil then reduce heat to low, cover and simmer for another 5 minutes. Gradually stir in the yoghurt until heated through.

Scallops with Garlic Parsley Sauce

4 thick slices Italian bread, toasted
2 tablespoons butter
1 1/2 tablespoons olive oil
700g Hervey Bay scallops, rinsed and patted dry
4 cloves garlic, minced
1/2 cup white wine
2 tablespoons lemon juice
1/4 cup chopped fresh flat-leaf parsley
4 tablespoons cold butter, cut into cubes
1 pinch cayenne pepper
Salt and ground black pepper to taste

Spread 1/2 tablespoon butter on one side of each piece of toasted Italian bread. Set aside.

Heat olive oil in a skillet over high heat. When oil begins to smoke, pour scallops into pan. Cook for 30 seconds without stirring.

Toss scallops in pan and stir in garlic. Cook and stir until fragrant, about 30 seconds.

Stir wine and lemon juice into scallops, bring to a boil, and cook for about 30 seconds.

Stir parsley and cold butter into scallops and remove from heat. When butter melts, stir in salt, black pepper, and cayenne pepper.

Spoon scallops over buttered toast and serve immediately.

Craig's Devillish Diavolo Linguine

A personal favourite and great with a good shiraz.

4 tablespoons olive oil, divided
6 cloves garlic, crushed
3 cups whole peeled tomatoes with liquid, chopped
1 1/2 teaspoons salt
1 teaspoon crushed red pepper flakes
1 pack linguine pasta
250g small prawns, peeled and de-veined
250g bay scallops
1 tablespoon chopped fresh parsley

In a large saucepan, heat 2 tablespoons of the olive oil with the garlic over medium heat. When the garlic starts to sizzle, pour in the tomatoes. Season with salt and red pepper. Bring to a boil. Lower the heat, and simmer for 30 minutes, stirring occasionally.

Meanwhile, bring a large pot of lightly salted water to a boil. Cook pasta for 8 to 10 minutes, drain.

In a large skillet, heat the remaining 2 tablespoons of olive oil over high heat. Add the shrimp and scallops. Cook for about 2 minutes, stirring frequently, or until the shrimp turn pink.

Add shrimp and scallops to the tomato mixture, and stir in the parsley. Cook for 3 to 4 minutes, or until the sauce just begins to bubble. Serve sauce over pasta.

Garlic Parmesan Crusted Scallops

1/2 cup bread crumbs
1/4 cup grated Parmesan cheese
1 teaspoon dried parsley
1/2 teaspoon garlic salt
1/2 teaspoon ground black pepper
1/2 cup olive oil
16 Hervey Bay scallops

Mix bread crumbs, Parmesan cheese, parsley, garlic salt, and black pepper together in a bowl.
Pour olive oil into a shallow bowl.

Rinse scallops under cold water, then dip into the olive oil.

Press scallops into bread crumb mixture. Gently toss between your hands so any bread crumbs that haven't stuck can fall away. Place the breaded scallops onto a plate while breading the rest.

Place the scallops in the refrigerator to allow the breading to set, 20 to 30 minutes.

Preheat an outdoor grill for medium-high heat, and lightly oil the grate.

Brush the scallops lightly with more olive oil.

Grill on the preheated grill until golden brown on both sides, about 5 minutes.

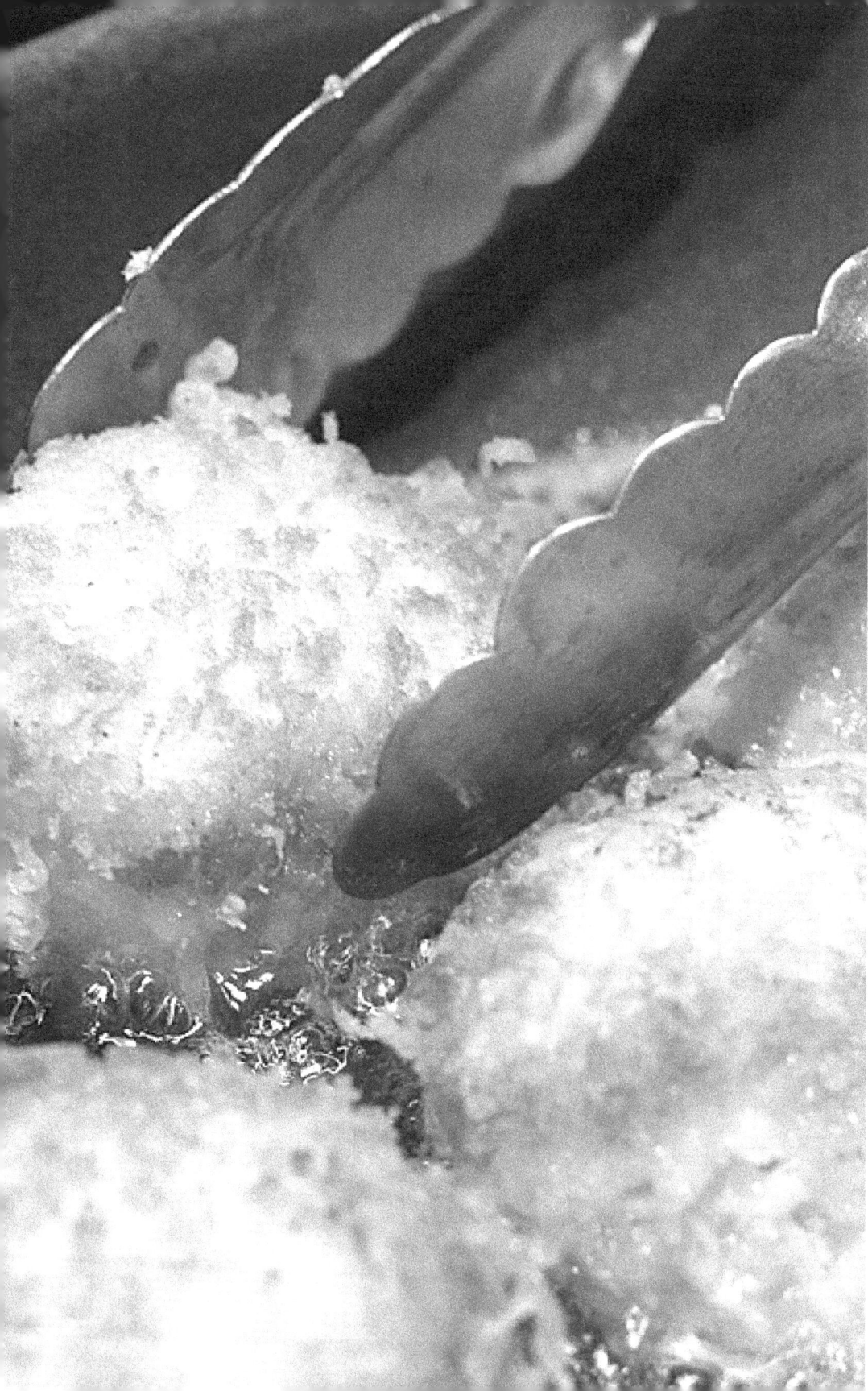

Crispy Red Emperor
with Thai Pumpkin Salad

4 fillets of red emperor, skin on
Sea salt
Cracked pepper
Oil for the barbecue

SALAD
500g pumpkin, 1/2 cm slices
1/2 bunch of coriander, washed, leaves picked
1 stick of lemongrass, sliced finely
1/4 cup of shallots, finely sliced
1 long red chilli, deseeded and finely sliced
100ml vegetable oil
2 limes, juiced
Limes wedges for garnish

Dry the fish fillet flesh and skin and sprinkle both sides with salt and pepper.

On a flat grill, medium-high heat, barbecue fillets skin side down for 7 minutes then turn and barbecue for a further two minutes.

Barbecue pumpkin slices for three minutes each side.

Place the pumpkin slices in a bowl and mix with coriander, lemongrass, shallots and chilli.

Mix oil and lime juice, then toss all salad ingredients together.

Arrange salad on four plates and top with red emperor.

Craig's Fijian Prawn Linguine

*I grew up in Fiji, a melting pot of nationalities where French restaurants served
pizza, where pizza restaurants served kebabs, and where Italian restaurants served
something a little like this...*

450g linguine pasta
1/2 cup olive oil
1/2 cup pineapple juice
1/2 cup pulp-free orange juice
5 teaspoons grated orange zest
5 teaspoons lemon zest
1 teaspoon salt
1 teaspoon pepper
5 cloves garlic, peeled
450g medium prawns - peeled and de-veined
2 tablespoons chopped fresh parsley
2 tablespoons grated Parmesan cheese

Fill a large pot with lightly salted water and bring to a rolling boil over high heat. Stir in
the linguine and return to a boil. Cook until the pasta is cooked through but is still firm
to the bite, about 11 minutes.

While pasta is cooking, combine the olive oil, pineapple juice, orange juice, orange
zest, lemon zest, salt, pepper and garlic in a blender. Blend on high speed until
smooth.

Pour sauce into a large frypan over medium-high heat. Bring to a simmer and cook
for 2 minutes. Add the prawns and parsley; cook until prawns are pink and cooked
through, 3 to 5 minutes.

Drain the linguine, and place on a serving platter. Spoon the prawns and sauce over
the pasta, and top with a sprinkle of Parmesan cheese.

World's Laziest Fish Cakes

3 cups mashed potato
200g tin of tuna, or leftover fish
1 onion, finely chopped
1 egg, beaten
Plain flour

Mix the potato, tuna and onion together, roll mixture into balls and flatten into patties.

Coat with egg and flour, then lightly fry in a little oil both sides until brown.

Serve with a summer salad, or eat as a snack.

Red Emperor Baked in Salt Dough

This dish will certainly impress the diners at your next dinner party, or equally when roughing it at a camp site.

1 x 3.5kg red emperor, scaled, gilled and gutted
Freshly ground black pepper, to taste
1 lemon, sliced
1 brown onion, sliced
6 sprigs flat-leaf parsley
6 sprigs dill
Steamed baby potatoes, to serve
Green salad with vinaigrette dressing, to serve

SALT DOUGH
1.5kg flour
1.2kg table salt
1.5 litres water

Make the Salt Dough: combine the flour and salt in a large bowl. Add ¾ of the water and mix well, if it is too dry, add extra water to bring the dough together, it should be quite firm. Tip the dough onto a lightly floured surface and knead until smooth. Wrap in plastic wrap and refrigerate for 30 minutes.
Preheat the oven to 210°C.

Lightly flour the bench and roll out the dough to a 1cm-thick rectangle.

Rinse the belly cavity of the fish and pat dry with paper towel. Sprinkle cavity well with pepper and place lemon, onion, parsley and dill inside. Place the fish in the centre of the dough and wrap it up, pinching together any cracks or seams.

Place on a baking paper-lined baking tray and cook for about 40 minutes, until the pastry has set and begun to colour. Remove from oven and rest in a warm place for at least 45 minutes.

Break open the dough at the table and gently spoon the fish onto plates. Serve with steamed potatoes and a green salad.

Sweet Potato, Spinach & Cashew Curry

Make this for dinner and even dedicated meat-eaters will thank you!

1/2 teaspoon cardamom seeds
4 whole peppercorns
1 teaspoon cumin seeds
1 teaspoon coriander seeds
1 teaspoon mustard seeds
Pinch chilli flakes
2 teaspoons ground turmeric
2 tablespoons peanut oil
1 onion, finely chopped
2 cloves garlic, crushed
6cm piece ginger, grated
600g orange sweet potato, cut into 2cm pieces
1 cup coconut milk
1 cup vegetable stock
1 cup toasted cashews
150g baby spinach leaves

Put cardamom, peppercorns, cumin, coriander, mustard seeds and chilli flakes in a dry frying pan over medium heat. Cook, stirring for 3 minutes. Remove from heat.

Spoon spices and turmeric into a spice grinder and grind to a powder.

Heat a non-stick frying pan over medium heat. Add oil, onion, garlic and ginger. Cook, stirring for 2 minutes.

Add sweet potato and toss in spice mixture.

Add coconut milk and stock and bring to the boil.

Reduce heat and simmer, partially covered, for 12 to 15 minutes or until sweet potato is tender.

Just before serving, add spinach and cashews and toss for 1 minute.

Chickpeas & Tomato Nut Sauce

A beautiful high protein, low fat vegetarian meal to serve with vegetables or rice.

400g can diced or crushed tomatoes
1 onion, diced
1 garlic clove
1 teaspoon cumin
1/2 teaspoon salt
1 cup water
1/2 cup almonds
1 teaspoon peanut butter
1 tablespoon soy sauce
1 tablespoon honey
425g can chickpeas, drained

Fry onion and garlic in a small amount of olive oil.

Add cumin and salt, then add tomatoes and simmer until thickened.

Blend remaining ingredients except chickpeas in a blender and add to tomato mixture.

Add chickpeas and simmer until thick.

Beer Battered Chips

6 large potatoes, scrubbed and cut into wedges
Vegetable oil, for deep frying
2 cups plain flour
Can of beer
Lemon pepper and salt, to season

Steam or microwave potatoes for approximately 15 minutes until tender.

Arrange wedges on trays in a single layer and freeze for 2 hours or until firm.

Heat oil over a high heat or use a deep fryer and heat until temperature reaches 180°C. Once oil is hot, whisk half the flour with the beer until just combined, don't overwork.

Dust wedges with remaining flour, then dip into batter. Deep fry wedges in batches until golden and crisp.

Serve with salt and lemon pepper.

Vegetarian Bolognaise Sauce

4 tablespoons olive oil
1 large onion, very finely chopped
3 1/2 cups mushrooms, very finely chopped
1 large garlic clove, crushed
425g can tomatoes
4 tablespoons red wine
4 tablespoons tomato paste
1 teaspoon dried basil or mixed herbs
1 teaspoon pitted and mashed olives (optional)
Salt and freshly ground black pepper, to taste

Heat oil in saucepan and fry onion, covered, for 5 minutes.

Add garlic and chopped mushrooms to the onion in pan, mix
and fry for a further 5
minutes, browning lightly and stirring often.

Add tomatoes, wine, tomato paste and basil or herbs.

Mix well, then cover and simmer for 25-30 minutes or until
thick and tasty. Season with
salt and pepper.

Serve with spaghetti and parmesan/romano cheese or freeze
in portions.

Zucchini Fritters

Feel free to throw a half cup of corn kernels into this recipe for some added sweetness. Perfect with freshly roasted chicken but equally as good on their own.

3 medium zucchini
1/2 cup self-raising flour
1/2 cup parmesan, finely grated
3 shallots, ends trimmed, thinly sliced
1 egg, whisked
1/4 cup fresh continental parsley, chopped
2 teaspoon dried oregano leaves
1 teaspoon salt
1/4 teaspoon ground nutmeg
4 teaspoon olive oil

Trim the ends from zucchini then coarsely grate. Place in a colander and squeeze out as much excess moisture as possible. Transfer to a bowl. Stir in self-raising flour, parmesan, shallots, egg, parsley, oregano, salt and nutmeg.

Heat the olive oil in a non-stick frying pan over medium-high heat. Drop four 2-tablespoonful measures of zucchini mixture into pan and cook for 1 $^1/_2$ minutes each side or until golden and cooked through.

Transfer to a plate lined with paper towel then repeat with remaining mixture.

Vegetarian Rissotto

1 large onion, diced
2 cloves garlic, crushed
2 medium carrots, finely diced
2 large zucchini, finely diced
6 large mushrooms, finely diced
1 broccoli floret, finely diced
1 cup finely diced cauliflower
1 cup frozen sweet corn kernels and peas
6 string beans, diced
2 fresh tomatoes, finely diced
1/4 cup fresh grated Parmesan cheese
1 cup reduced fat grated tasty cheese
1 x 190g jar sun dried tomato pesto
Salt and pepper, to taste
2 tablespoons powdered vegetable stock
2 litres water
2 tablespoons olive oil
3-4 cups long grain rice

In a heavy based, large pot, heat olive oil and gently fry garlic and onion together, stirring so the garlic does not catch.

Add rice and stir to coat.

Add pesto and stir thoroughly.

Add all other vegetables except peas and corn and stir then add half of water with dissolved stock and tomatoes.

Stir well, cover with lid and reduce heat to a slow bubble.

Continue adding stock as it is absorbed, stirring well. When risotto has absorbed the stock, add frozen peas and corn.

Add Parmesan and tasty grated cheese and stir well.

Season to taste.

Classic French Onion Soup

This is a sensation but for best effect I suggest it be served with the suggested Gruyere...bonne nourriture!

80g butter
4 large brown onions, sliced into rings
2 garlic cloves, crushed
2 teaspoons plain flour
6 cups beef stock
1/2 cup dry red wine
1 bouquet garni sachet
Salt & freshly ground black pepper
30cm French stick cut crossways into slices
1 cup finely shredded Gruyere cheese

Heat the butter in a large saucepan over medium heat. Add the onions and garlic and stir for 10 minutes or until the onions are soft and light golden. Add the flour and stir for 1 minute or until flour bubbles and comes away from the side of the pan.

Add the stock, wine and bouquet garni. Bring to the boil over medium-high heat. Reduce heat to low and simmer, uncovered, stirring occasionally, for 30 minutes or until soup thickens slightly. Remove bouquet garni. Taste and season with salt and pepper.

Preheat grill on high. Place baguette slices on a baking tray. Place under preheated grill and cook for 2 minutes each side or until light golden. Remove from grill and sprinkle each slice evenly with the cheese. Place under grill and cook for a further 2 minutes or until the cheese melts. Sit one or two of these in the top of each bowl of soup.

Potato & Leek Soup

1/4 cup olive oil
1 brown onion, halved, chopped
1 garlic clove, crushed
4 medium (about 700g) peeled potatoes, cubed
2 leeks, pale section only, washed, dried, thinly sliced
5 cups vegetable stock
3 thick slices day-old white bread, cubed
1/2 cup thickened cream
Pinch of salt
2 tablespoons finely chopped fresh chives

Heat 1 tablespoon of the oil in a large saucepan over medium-high heat. Add the onion and garlic and cook,
stirring, for 3 minutes or until the onion softens. Add the potato and leek and cook, stirring, for 5 minutes or until leek softens.

Add the stock and bring to the boil. Reduce heat to medium and gently boil, uncovered, for 20 minutes
or until potato is soft. Remove from heat and set aside for 10 minutes to cool.

Meanwhile, preheat oven to 180°C. Place bread in a roasting pan. Drizzle with remaining oil and toss
until bread is evenly coated. Toast in preheated oven, shaking pan occasionally, for 10 minutes or until crisp. Remove croutons from oven and set aside.
Transfer one-third of the potato mixture to the jug of a blender and blend until smooth. Transfer to a clean saucepan. Repeat in 2 more batches with the remaining potato mixture.

Place the soup over medium heat. Add the cream and stir to combine. Cook, stirring, for 5 minutes or until hot. Taste and season with salt.

Ladle the soup among serving bowls. Sprinkle with chives and top with croutons. Serve immediately.

TOP TIP
This soup will keep in an airtight container in the fridge for up to 3 days.

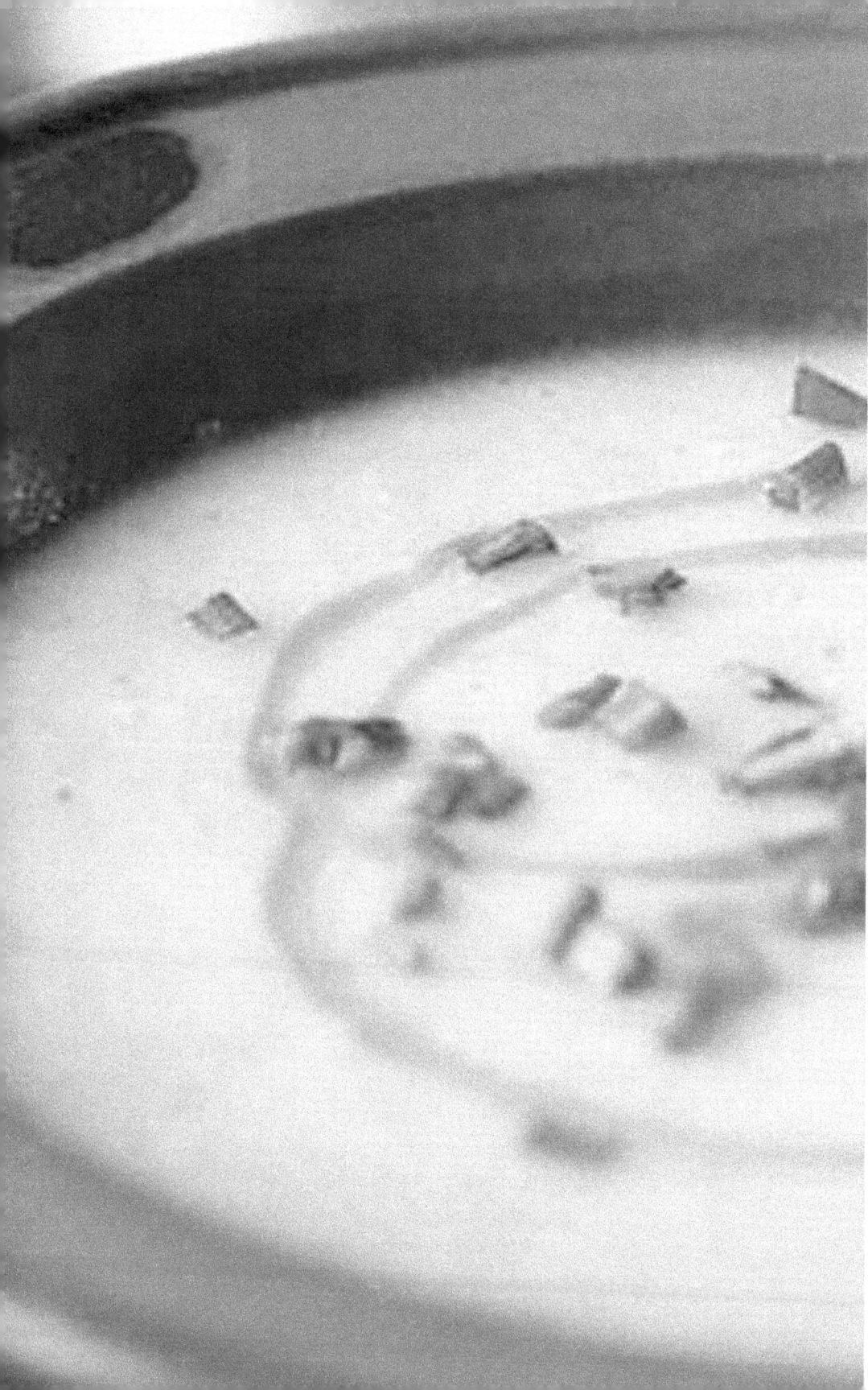

Confetti Salad

Light and colourful for summer BBQs.

4 cups cooked rice
1 bunch of asparagus, cooked and diced
1/2 cup green peas, slightly cooked
3 slices of red capsicum, diced
1/2 cup chopped parsley
2 spring onions, diced
400g can 4 bean mix, drained
200g can corn kernels
Pepper
2 tablespoons herbed vinegar
Diced cucumber (optional)
Diced chilli (optional)

Mix all ingredients together.

Keep cool until served.

Vegetarian Lasagne

1 onion, chopped
3 cloves garlic
2 tablespoons olive oil
1 eggplant, diced
1 large zucchini, diced
4 roasted capsicums
400g can chopped tomatoes
2 x 420g jars tomato pasta sauce
Fresh lasagne sheets
500g tub ricotta
1 1/2 cups grated cheddar cheese
1/2 cup shaved Parmesan cheese
Chilli powder, to taste
Italian herbs, to taste

In a large pan, cook onion and garlic in oil until soft. Add eggplant and zucchini and cook until softened.

Add roasted capsicums, tomatoes, pasta sauce, chilli powder, salt, pepper, Italian herbs and 1/2 cup water, and simmer for 30 minutes.

Preheat oven to 180°C.

Grease baking dish and layer with 1/5 vegetable mix, followed by lasagne sheets and 1/4 ricotta cheese. Repeat 4 times then top with last of the vegetable mix and add cheddar and Parmesan cheese.

Bake for 40 minutes or until brown.

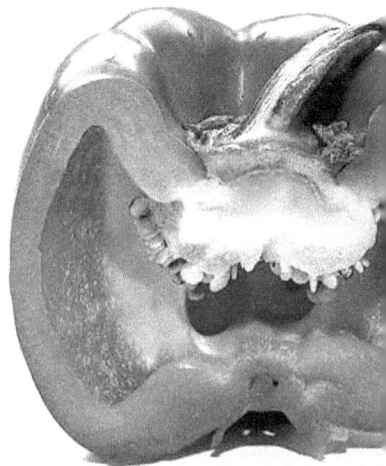

Flower-child Nachos

Meat-free and super tasty!

1 tablespoon olive oil
1 medium brown onion, finely chopped
2 garlic cloves, finely chopped
1/4 teaspoon ground chillies
400g can diced tomatoes
450g can vegetarian refried beans
125ml vegetable stock
400g can red kidney beans, drained, rinsed
250g block cheddar cheese, grated
230g packet original corn chips
1 large ripe avocado, peeled and mashed
1/3 cup light sour cream

Fry onion, garlic and ground chillies in large saucepan over medium heat. Cover and cook, stirring occasionally, for 5 minutes or until the onions are softened.

Add tomatoes, refried beans and stock; stir to combine.
Bring to the boil and then simmer, uncovered, stirring occasionally for 15 minutes. Stir in the kidney beans.

Preheat oven to 200°C.

Sprinkle a little cheese over the base of 4 ovenproof dishes. Spoon the bean mixture evenly over the cheese then arrange the corn chips over the top and sprinkle with the remaining cheese.

Bake for 5 minutes or until the cheese has melted.

Combine avocado and sour cream in a small bowl.

Remove the nachos from the oven, top with the avocado mixture and serve immediately.

Tasty Vegetable Pasta

400g dry pasta
400g tin diced or crushed tomatoes
2 cups vegetable stock
200ml water
4 medium mushrooms, sliced
1 medium zucchini, diced
1 stalk celery, diced
1 cup frozen corn
400g tin chickpeas, thoroughly rinsed
1/4 onion, diced, or frozen onion
1 teaspoon crushed garlic
1 tablespoon cornflour, made into a paste with 2 tablespoons water
Black pepper, to taste
Oregano, to taste
Olive oil

Heat oil and sauté garlic and onion until onion is clear.

Add vegetables and sauté for a further 5 minutes, stirring. Add stock, tomatoes and water. Stir, and bring to simmering point. Add chickpeas, and simmer for 5 minutes.

Add corn, black pepper and oregano and bring back to simmering point. Add cornflour mixture, stirring continuously. Simmer for 15 minutes, stirring frequently. While sauce is cooking, prepare pasta, drain then mix pasta into sauce and serve.

Sausage(less) Rolls

Everyone loves sausage rolls...except for vegetarians, but with this meatless version of the classic hot pastry, now even they can.

1 tablespoon olive oil
1 onion, chopped
2 x 400g cans brown lentils, drained and rinsed
1/4 cup barbeque sauce
1/2 cup chopped pecans
1/2 cup dry breadcrumbs
2 tablespoons chopped parsley
3 sheets puff pastry
2 tablespoons sesame or any other seeds
Soy milk, for brushing

Fry the onion until golden, set aside. Allow to cool.

Stir through the lentils, sauce, pecans, breadcrumbs and parsley. Sprinkle each sheet of pastry with half of the seeds.

Cut pastry sheets in half, fill with mixture, brush edges with a little soy milk or water and roll up, as for sausage rolls then brush with soy milk and sprinkle over the remaining sesame seeds.

Cut each roll in half or into 6 party size pieces.

Bake at 200°C for 30 minutes.

Egg White Quiche

Low fat, low carb, dairy free, vegetarian and high protein quiche

2 carrots, grated
1 zucchini, grated
12 egg whites
Spray oil
Spinach, to taste
1/2 broccoli, diced
Salt, to taste

Pre-heat oven to 200°C and grease a cake pan with spray oil.

In a bowl, whisk egg whites and add a pinch of salt.

Add all the vegetables, mix well and pour into cake tin.

Bake for 20 minutes or until the egg is completely cooked.

The Forget-me-not Eco-Village is being constructed on 27,000 square metres of land in Nepal purchased by the Forget-me-not Foundation, and will eventually support 60 orphans and employ 15 local Nepali staff.

Brainchild of Hervey Bay Sunrise Rotarian and Forget-me-not CEO Lars Olsen , the Eco Village is now our chief RAWCS project and has seen many Rotarians visit and assist with all facets of construction, from the building of stone retaining walls, to the building and finishing of the housing pods and amenities blocks.

Want to know more about this major project? Get in contact with us and we'll let you know the many different ways you can be involved.

cakes, bakes and desserts

Henny's Strawberry Flummery with Strawberry Coulis

1 can of evaporated milk
1 packet of jelly (raspberry or strawberry)
1 punnet of strawberries
Small amount of cherry brandy (or water if you're not into booze)
After dinner mint sticks
1 teaspoon caster sugar

Refrigerate milk for 24 hours.

Make up jelly with only half the normal amount of water and cool until just wobbly

Beat both milk and jelly in separate bowls until frothy then mix together carefully and place in individual ramekins and refrigerate until set. Preferably overnight.

Meanwhile keeping a few strawberries aside with stems intact place the rest of the cleaned strawberries in a blender with sugar and a very small amount of Cherry Brandy. Blend to a smooth slurry. Once Strawberry Flummery is set, use a warm damp cloth to wipe around each ramekin and upend onto a nice dessert plate.

Drizzle Strawberry Coulis over top of Flummery and decorate with a half strawberry that's been sliced and fanned and an after dinner mint stick.

This recipe is also a real favourite with children. In this case instead of ramekins, just let the whole lot set in a large bowl and serve with ice cream, and strawberry or chocolate sauce. Needless to say leave out the booze.

Doreen's Marvellous Muffins

2 cups self-raising flour
3/4 cup of skim milk
3/4 cup of caster or low GI sugar
2 eggs lightly beaten
1/2 cup light olive oil
1 teaspoon of natural vanilla extract
1 cup of fresh or frozen raspberries, blackberries etc

Sift the flour into a bowl, and stir in the sugar. Make a well in the middle of dry ingredients.

Beat together, in a separate bowl, the oil, eggs, milk and vanilla.

Pour the mixture into the well in the dry ingredients.

Add the berries and lightly fold together until blended.

Place 12 muffin size cake cases in a muffin tray. Lightly spray with oil.

Spoon the mixture into cases filled to two-thirds.

Place in a pre-heated oven to 190 or 200°C and cook for approximately 20 minutes. Ovens vary and so use a skewer to check on readiness. Remove from pan after cooled for two minutes. These freeze well.

You can use other fillings like sultanas, chocolate chips, and crystallized ginger. Omit sugar, and vanilla and use shredded cheese, ham and a teaspoon of mild curry powder for savoury muffins.

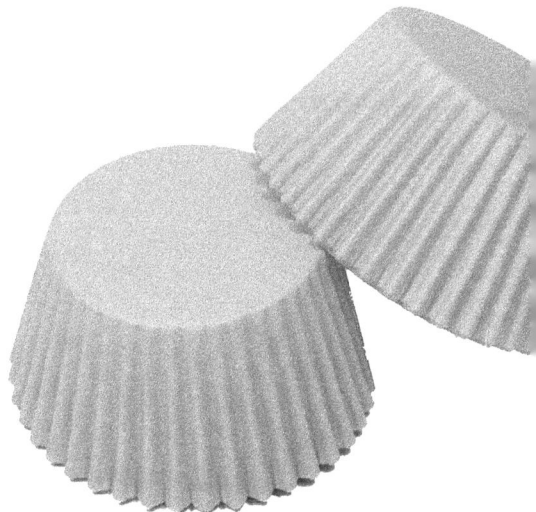

Andy's Bloody Good Carrot Cake

1 1/2 cups of finely grated carrot
3/4 cup of sultanas or raisins
3/4 cup of chopped walnuts or almonds
1/4 teaspoon of salt
1 teaspoon of cinnamon or nutmeg
3/4 cup of macadamia or light olive oil
2 eggs lightly beaten
1 cup of raw brown sugar
2/3 cup of self-raising flour
1/3 cup of plain flour

CREAM FROSTING
250 grams of light cream cheese softened
1/4 cup of butter or margarine softened
1/4 cup of icing sugar, sifted
I teaspoon of natural vanilla extract

Mix together carrot, dried fruit, nuts, salt, and spice in a large bowl. Add the sifted flour.

In a saucepan gently warm sugar. Turn off and add oil and ginger. Add beaten eggs.

Place liquid ingredients into the bowl with other ingredients and stir well. Pour into a greased and lined cake tin.

Pre-heat oven to 180°C. Cook for approx. 40 mins. Use the skewer test to see if cooked.

Let it cool before adding frosting, which is optional, but delicious!!

Frosting
Beat cream cheese, butter or margarine, icing sugar, and vanilla together. Cool in fridge.
Spread over cake top and sides with a flat knife. Decorate with sprinkles, nuts etc.
Enjoy!

Lazy White Chocolate Mud Cake

200g butter
200g white chocolate
1 1/4 cups caster sugar
3/4 cups water
1 teaspoon vanilla essence
1 cup plain flour
1 cup self-raising flour
2 eggs, lightly beaten

CHOCOLATE GANACHE
200g white chocolate
1/4 cup cream

Melt butter, chocolate, sugar and water over gentle heat. Stir in vanilla. Cool to room temperature. Sift dry ingredients into a bowl. Add beaten eggs to chocolate mixture, then fold in sifted dry ingredients. Pour into lined 20-22cm round cake tin and bake at 160°C until cooked when tested.

Cool in tin.

Make chocolate ganache by melting chocolate with cream. Cool slightly before spreading over cake. Allow to set overnight.

Tiramisu for Cheats

500g fresh ricotta
1/4 cup caster sugar
1/4 cup coffee-flavoured liqueur
80g dark chocolate, finely chopped
1/2 x 460g packaged double unfilled sponge
1/2 cup espresso coffee, cooled
2/3 cup icing sugar mixture
1 tablespoon cocoa powder, sifted
1 teaspoon butter, softened
1 1/2 tablespoons milk
Shaved dark chocolate, to serve

Using an electric mixer, beat ricotta, sugar and liqueur for 2 minutes or until smooth. Stir in chocolate.

Using a serrated knife, cut cake horizontally into thirds. Place base on a plate. Brush with 1/3 of the coffee. Spread with 1/2 the ricotta. Place middle layer of cake on ricotta. Brush with 1/2 of the remaining espresso. Spread with remaining ricotta mixture. Brush cut side of sponge top with remaining coffee. Place over ricotta mixture, cut-side down.

Combine icing sugar and cocoa in a small bowl. Make a well in centre. Add butter and milk. Stir until combined. Spread over cake. Refrigerate for 1 hour. Sprinkle with shaved chocolate. Serve.

Coconut Citrus Balls

Melted butter, to grease
1 tablespoon desiccated coconut
3/4 cup self-raising flour
1/4 cup Equal Spoonfuls (Equal brand)
1 teaspoon zested orange rind
1 teaspoon zested lemon rind
1/2 cup skim milk
1 egg white, lightly whisked
1 tablespoon butter, melted

Preheat oven to 180°C. Brush 12 (20ml/1 tbs) round-based patty pans with the melted butter to lightly grease. Place the coconut in a small non-stick frying pan over medium heat and cook, stirring, for 1 minute or until lightly toasted. Transfer to a small bowl and set aside.

Sift the flour and Equal Spoonfuls into a medium bowl. Add the orange and lemon zest, and stir to combine. Make a well in the centre.

Whisk milk, egg white and butter in a small jug until well combined. Add to flour mixture and stir to combine. Divide mixture evenly among greased pans. Sprinkle coconut evenly over top. Bake in preheated oven for 15 minutes or until golden and a skewer inserted in the centres comes out clean.

Remove the citrus coconut balls from the oven and set aside for 2 minutes. Transfer to a wire rack for a further 3 minutes. Serve warm.

Craig's Famous Five-Minute Gelati

There is nothing politically correct about this recipe...
it's all to do with flavour and nothing to do with diets!

2 cups regular whipping cream
1 cup castor sugar
1/4 cup orange cordial
1/2 teaspoon salt

Whisk it all together until the cream is ALMOST whipped (but not quite), pour it into a container and freeze for at least eight hours, ideally overnight.

That's it. Yes, really!

Substitute the orange cordial for almost anything...crushed chocolate cookies, watermelon pieces, grapefruit, whatever you like. Feel free to add a drop of food colouring for added pizazz!

Bread & Butter Pudding

7-9 slices bread
100g raisins
100g soft brown sugar
3 eggs
500ml milk
2 apples, cored and sliced
5 tablespoons orange marmalade
Cinnamon
Nutmeg
Butter

Preheat oven to 180°C and lightly grease a baking dish with butter.

Place apples and half the sugar into a bowl, coat apples with sugar and pour into prepared
dish.

Spread butter and jam on bread. Use half the bread to cover the apples.

Sprinkle half the raisins and 2 tablespoons of sugar over the bread.

Beat eggs and milk together and pour half over the bread in the dish.

Press remaining raisins into the leftover bread and place into the dish.

Pour the remaining egg mixture over the top and sprinkle with cinnamon, nutmeg and
remaining sugar.

Let rest for 30 minutes.

Bake for 45 minutes to 1 hour until well risen and golden brown.

Serve hot or cold.

Jane's Spanish Apple Cake

250g brown sugar
250g butter (not margarine)
4 large eggs
250g self raising flour, sifted
60g desicated coconut
500g cooled stewed apples (you can use tin pie apples if you like they work just as well)

Pre heat oven to 180°C, then grease and line an 20cm round cake tin.

Cream butter and sugar till light and fluffy. Add eggs one at a time mixing well between each addition then with a metal spoon fold in flour, coconut and lastly the stewed apples.

Place in moderate oven and cook for 1 to 1 1/2 hr.
Cake should be golden in colour and the skewer should come out clean.

Cool in the tin before turning out.

This is a deliciously moist cake and is great served warm with whipped cream as a dessert.

Berry Honeycomb Ice Cream Terrine

2 punnets fresh raspberries
2.5 litres good quality vanilla ice cream
2 x 50g chocolate coated honeycomb bars
Extra raspberries, to serve

Line a 20cm cake pan with plastic wrap. Place in the freezer until required.

Spoon half the ice cream into a large bowl and set aside to soften slightly. Return the remaining ice cream to the freezer.

Put the raspberries in a bowl and use a fork to roughly mash. Fold the raspberries through the softened ice cream. Spoon into the lined pan and smooth the surface. Freeze for about 2 hours, until firm.

Break the honeycomb bar into chunks and place into a plastic bag. Use a rolling pin to smash the chunks. Place the remaining ice cream in a bowl and soften slightly. Fold in the honeycomb. Spoon over the raspberry ice cream, and smooth the surface. Freeze for 2 hours, until firm.

Turn out onto a chilled platter. Scatter with extra raspberries to serve.

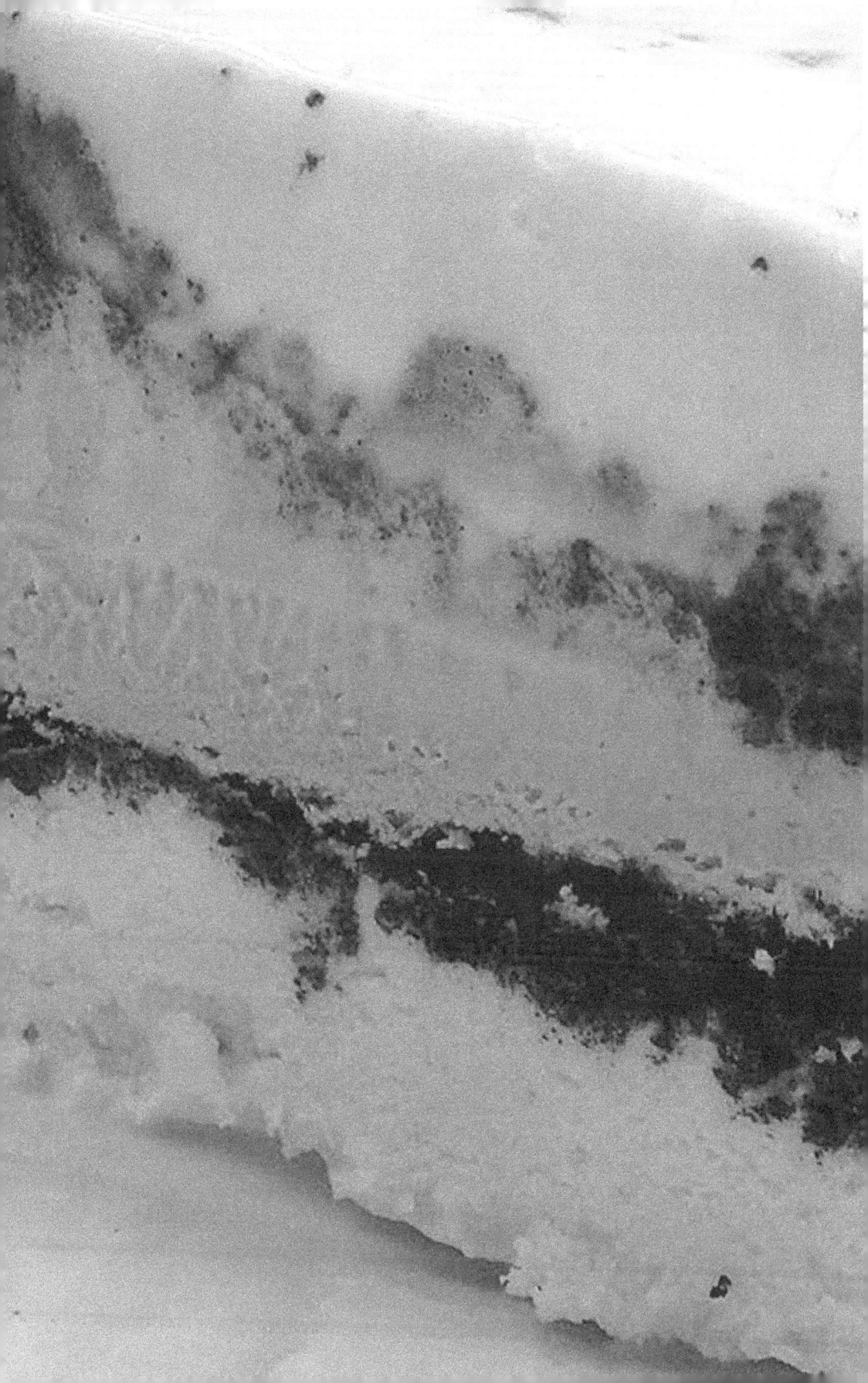

Golden Syrup Dumplings

A very easy winter favourite.

1 cup self-raising flour
60g unsalted butter, cubed
1 egg
1-2 tablespoons of milk, to beat
Thick cream, to serve

SYRUP
30g butter
1 cup caster sugar
4 tablespoons golden syrup
1 small lemon, juiced

Sift flour into a bowl, then rub in butter until mixture resembles fine breadcrumbs. Beat egg with a little milk and pour into flour mixture. Combine to form a dough, then divide into small balls.

To make the syrup, combine the ingredients together with 1 cup of water in a pan and bring to the boil over medium heat. Carefully add dough balls to syrup and boil for 20 minutes. Serve with syrup and cream.

Self-Saucing Chocolate Pudding

1 cup self-raising flour
2 tablespoons cocoa powder
1/2 cup brown sugar
80g butter, melted, cooled
1/2 cup milk
1 egg, lightly beaten
Thick cream and berries, to serve

SAUCE
3/4 cup brown sugar
2 tablespoons cocoa powder, sifted
1 1/4 cups boiling water

Preheat oven to 180°C. Grease an 8-cup capacity ovenproof baking dish. Sift flour and cocoa into a large bowl. Stir in sugar.

Combine butter, milk and egg in a jug. Slowly add to flour mixture, whisking until well combined and smooth. Spoon into baking dish. Smooth top.

Make sauce: Sprinkle combined sugar and cocoa over pudding.

Slowly pour boiling water over the back of a large metal spoon to cover pudding. Place dish onto a baking tray. Bake for 35 to 40 minutes or until pudding bounces back when pressed gently in centre.

Serve hot with cream and berries.

Craig's Vanilla Custard Tarts

24 wonton wrappers
2 teaspoons caster sugar

CUSTARD
1/3 cup caster sugar
2 1/2 tablespoons custard powder
2 cups reduced-fat milk
2 teaspoons vanilla essence
150g cherries, quartered, stones removed
2 teaspoons pure icing sugar, to serve

Preheat oven to 180°C. Grease a 12-hole, 1/3-cup capacity muffin pan. Lightly brush 1 wonton wrapper with cold water and sprinkle with a little sugar. Place another wrapper on top crossways (so it looks like a star). Ease pastry into 1 muffin hole. Repeat with remaining wrappers and sugar. Bake tart cases for 15 minutes or until crisp and golden. Allow to cool in pan.

Make custard: Combine sugar and custard powder in a medium saucepan. Gradually add milk, whisking constantly until smooth. Add vanilla. Place over low heat. Cook, stirring, for 5 to 10 minutes or until custard boils and thickens. Remove from heat. Cover surface of custard with plastic wrap. Allow to cool for 15 minutes.

Half-fill tart cases with custard. Refrigerate for 3 hours or until set. Top with cherries. Dust with icing sugar. Serve.

Strawberry & Mascarpone Wafers

2 x 250g punnets strawberries, hulled, halved
1/4 cup caster sugar
1 teaspoon vanilla extract
250g mascarpone cheese
1/4 cup thickened cream
1 tablespoon sifted icing sugar
12 Arnott's Lattice biscuits

Place strawberries, caster sugar and vanilla in a saucepan over medium-high heat and cook, stirring, for 1-2 minutes until the sugar has melted and the strawberries have just started to soften - don't overcook them, they still need to be firm.

Whisk together the mascarpone, cream and icing sugar. Place half the biscuits on serving plates, top each with a dollop of the mascarpone cream, followed by some of the strawberries, reserving any juices.

Top with the remaining biscuits and drizzle with the berry juices.

Lebanese Fruit Salad

A different way of looking at a classic Australian icon,
the humble fruit salad.

1 apple, core removed, diced
1 pear, core removed, diced
1 peach, stone removed, diced
1/3 cup dried apricots, chopped
1/3 cup dried figs, chopped
1/4 cup flaked almonds
1/4 cup shelled pistachio nuts
1 small lemon, rind zested
1 pinch ground cloves
1/2 teaspoon vanilla extract
1/2 cup apple juice
1 teaspoon rosewater essence
Vanilla ice-cream, to serve

TOPPING
1 tablespoon sugar
2 tablespoons shelled pistachio nuts, chopped
1 tablespoon cinnamon

Combine apple, pear, peach, apricots, figs and nuts in a large bowl. Mix well.

Add zest, cloves, vanilla, juice and rosewater to fruit mixture and mix well to combine.
Divide between 4 bowls top with ice-cream.

Make topping combining sugar, nuts and cinnamon. and sprinkle over ice-cream.

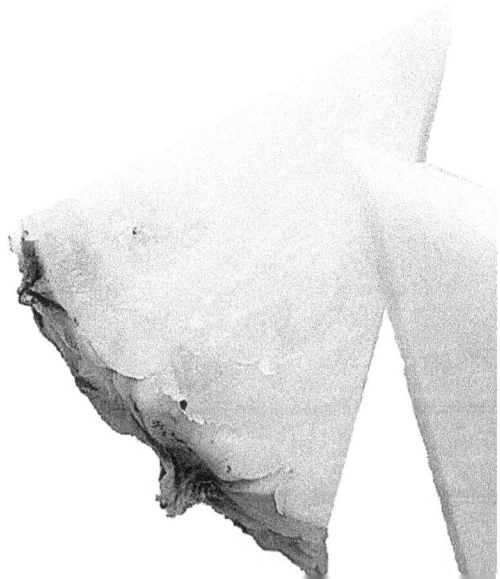

Toffee Melon Balls & Ginger Yoghurt

1 cup vanilla yoghurt
1 tablespoon finely chopped glacé ginger
1/4 rockmelon, seeded
1/4 honeydew melon, seeded
1/2 cup caster sugar

Combine yoghurt and ginger in a bowl.

Using a melon baller, scoop balls from rockmelon and honeydew melon. Place on a large plate lined with paper towel. Cover with paper towel and pat dry.

Combine caster sugar and 1/4 cup hot water in a small heavy-based saucepan over low heat. Cook, stirring, for 4 minutes or until sugar is dissolved. Increase heat to high. Bring to the boil. Boil, without stirring, for 8 minutes or until mixture turns golden. Set aside for 30 seconds for bubbles to subside.

Arrange melon balls in a large serving bowl. Drizzle over toffee. Stand at room temperature for 5 minutes or until toffee is set and cooled. Serve immediately with yoghurt mixture.

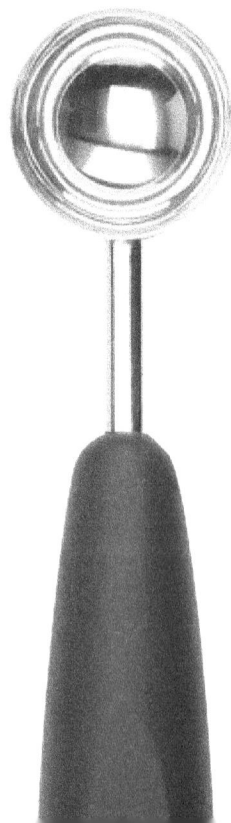

Caramelised Pineapple

Great with vanilla ice cream, and a host of other things. Simple, summery and delicious!

1/2 fresh pineapple, peeled, cut into 1cm thick slices
1 tablespoon brown sugar
20g butter
2 tablespoons Malibu coconut liqueur
Fresh passionfruit pulp, to serve

Sprinkle both sides of the pineapple with the sugar. Melt the butter in a non-stick frying pan over high heat until foaming and add the pineapple, cooking for 2 minutes each side or until golden brown.

Add the Malibu and bring to the boil. Remove from heat.

Divide pineapple among serving plates. Drizzle over with the pan juices and top with ice cream and passionfruit or your choice of other toppings.

What would it take to change the world? Rotary's 1.2 million members believe it starts with a commitment to Service Above Self.

In more than 33,000 clubs worldwide, you'll find members volunteering in communities at home and abroad to support education and job training, provide clean water, combat hunger, improve health and sanitation, and eradicate polio.

If you think you're one of us, feel free to approach a Rotarian about joining the first and strongest service club in the world. Sure, you need to be invited to join, but plenty of Rotarians will put their hand up to do just that if you tell us you're interested.

Rotary Clubs meet at different times each week, some - like ours - are breakfast clubs, whilst others meet at lunchtimes or dinner, so there is always going to be a Club that fits in with your schedule.

Each Club's President aims to make meetings quick, friendly and interesting, and while many of us do like to keep the Rotary traditions alive, meetings aren't bogged down with pomp and ceremony like you may think.

Most Clubs are a mix both men and women from all professions; business leaders and owners, managers and practitioners, and from all walks of life.

Rotary is neither politically nor religiously aligned.

www.rotaryaustralia.org.au

www.ingramcontent.com/pod-product-compliance
Lightning Source LLC
Chambersburg PA
CBHW030947090426
42737CB00007B/547